Slender Reeds

◆ ◆ ◆

Slender Reeds

◆ ◆ ◆

POEMS

Mirna Hirschl

DANCING LEAVES PRESS
2024

Copyright © 2024
Dancing Leavess Press
All Rights Reserved.

◆ ◆ ◆

Dancing Leaves Press
ISBN Number 978-1-7342742-6-4

Previously published in 2022:
How Memories Insist: Poems.

Cover image: *Slender Reeds* by Robert Perry, pencil drawing with indigo ink wash, 2024.

For our beloved grandchilden

André, Stéphane
Siena, Jason
Elena, Nikhil
Adam, Violet, Audrey

May we remember those of our family
who came before us, whom we learn about
in this book of poems dedicated to you
and their memory.

CONTENTS

❖ ❖ ❖

POEMS
   1   SLENDER REEDS

I. A ROSE-HIP FAIRY TALE

   5   A ROSE-HIP FAIRY TALE
   7   A CIRCLE
  10   WHAT BAKA SAID
  12   LIVING IN A BUTTERFLY WORLD
  14   BAKA'S HOUR
  15   BAKA ON AN ESCALATOR
  16   RAINY DAY CONCERTS
  18   ARTIFACT

II. THE BELOVED GHOSTS

  23   THEN, WHAT IS TRUE
  24   ETUŠ | ESTERA
  26   ROZA | RUŽA
  27   IZO | IZRAEL
  28   MARCI | MARTIN
  29   FANI | FRANCIKA
  30   ACO | ARMIN
  31   MARKICA | MARKO
  32   LINA AND JOSEF | JOSIP SANDBERG

III. EYES OF SILENCE

- 35   EYES OF SILENCE
- 36   SANCTUARY
- 37   MY OMAMA
- 38   DUMPLINGS AND PARSNIP ROOT
- 40   SACKS OF TAWNY WALNUTS
- 42   ROOTS OF CAUTION
- 43   POPPIES IN THE FALLOW FIELDS
- 44   WITNESSING A VOID
- 45   BOMBING FLARES

IV. C IS FOR CAMELLIA

- 49   C IS FOR CAMELLIA
- 50   NINA NANA
- 52   TEMPORARY BLISS
- 53   SCHERZO
- 54   PLAYING HOOKY
- 56   MEMENTO
- 57   BRIDGING AN ARROYO
- 58   THE THIRD PASSENGER
- 59   SIMPLY SAID, *AMARCORD*
- 60   WAITING FOR THE LIGHT

V. GALLERY OF PORTRAITS

- 63   I HAVE A BIRD FRIEND
- 64   TONY
- 66   A LILAC WORLD
- 68   MRS. KÖNIG WOULD HAVE BEEN A HUNDRED AND FIFTY YEARS OLD TODAY
- 70   THE LAST TIME I SAW MY FRIEND
- 72   FRAU ELSA
- 74   A CONFESSION AT 3 AM

VI. LANDSCAPES OF THE HEART

- 77   THE PIAZZA
- 80   HAMLET IN DUBROVNIK
- 82   UNDECIPHERED IN CAPUA
- 83   CANTO OF AN OLEANDER BUD
- 84   PAINTED NAILS
- 86   WAKE UP CALL
- 88   BEACH MINUET

VII. THE WAYWARD LOGIC OF DREAMS

- 91   TIEPOLO SKY
- 92   THE WAYWARD LOGIC OF DREAMS
- 94   FELLINI-ESQUE
- 96   SUNSET
- 98   ELVES OF HOPE
- 100   ON THE ROAD TO BANFF
- 101   ENTRANCED
- 102   IN THE LEOPOLD MUSEUM IN VIENNA
- 103   MOONSTONES AND A BIRD

VIII. SOFTLY AT DUSK

- 107   SONG OF THE CONCH
- 108   JANUS MASK
- 109   BARCAROLLE
- 110   SCENT OF SPRING
- 111   JUST IMAGINE
- 112   AUTUMN CONVERSATION
- 113   ROSE OF SHARON

IX. WHITE MOTH INTERLUDE

- 117   WHITE MOTH INTERLUDE
- 118   HOME TO OKAPI
- 119   ON A CLEAR DAY
- 120   A GLASS OF BUBBLY
- 122   COAXING WORDS
- 124   AN IMPASSE
- 125   HOURGLASS OF TRUTH

X. BAREFOOTED HOPE

- 129   BAREFOOTED HOPE
- 130   BLADE OF GRASS
- 132   THE KEY
- 134   SCENE FROM A PRIVATE MOVIE
- 136   PERPETUAL MOTION
- 137   CREDO

- 139   NOTES
- 142   ACKNOWLEDGEMENTS
- 144   COLOPHON

POEMS

♦ ♦ ♦

Slender Reeds

Dislocated, disconnected
itinerant

My cradle
a cartwheel of generations
never rooted, never anchored
combed the earth for
familiar faces in unfamiliar lands

How the mountain air sings!
How the salty expanse delights!

Pretending to have no weight
I float on a web of hopes
buoyant enough to uphold me
lofty enough to span continents

a creature for which fate invented
untried games

Oh Siddhartha
you who are not my Teacher by birth
help me find my river
steer my raft
of a single life-long glance
so that I may leave my children
the swaying of slender reeds

I.

A ROSE-HIP FAIRY TALE

In the forest of my childhood
sunrays toyed with shadows

A ROSE-HIP FAIRY TALE

In the forest of my childhood
sunrays toyed with shadows
on a briar rose bush floor

The roses have gifted fragrance
to the swollen, scarlet fruit
hiding on the brambly branches
warding off intruders

One sultry summer afternoon
we picked rose-hips and whispered
as we listened to the forest
which was there first

The leaves rustled in the tree tops
Sandals shuffled through
the sprawling underbrush
In the distance, the woodpeckers
pecked on oaks in rapid tap-taps

In this enchanted, simple world
everyone performed a role

I slid delicately
small hands through the thorny tangles
to harvest the fruit

My father carried heavy baskets
His whistling added to the chorus
of the perky robins chirping in the brush

My mother walked beside him silently
smiled as if she knew a grand secret
and waited her turn

Back home, we pressed the fruit
arduously, through a special sieve
A residue of tiny needles
embedded in fingers
prickled with accomplishment

Then my father lit the stove

My mother stirred a bubbling jam
in a pumpkin-yellow pan
until her wooden ladle-wand
drew the clear parting lines
over the enameled bottom

and the small room was enveloped
with the last breath of roses

This poem is written by the child I was
in memory of the breathing forest
playful sunrays that caressed
hunched shoulders of my family
and heavy baskets brimming
with sweetness and promise

A CIRCLE

A wedding ring
a plate's rounded lip
the route of a single day
a calendar dance

My life
my mother's life

A journey she took when
she married my father
until death did them part

I resemble him, not her—
an early blond turned brunette
hazel eyes, fine hair
always flying somewhere
weaving dust motes into stories

Like the rest of her
my mother's hair steady
black with a wavy sheen
eyes tender with a dark gleam

Their differences in temperaments
complemented each other

She, principled to the end
saw the world
through a black and white
kaleidoscope—
he and I preferred
the complexity of grays

She was deep, reserved
not easy to know
He and I wore our sentiments
as if they were clothing

My father liked to escape
into other people

My mother preferred
the refuge of books:
They were more reliable and kinder
who could blame her
she lost all four of her siblings
to the obscenities of World War Two

I regret I didn't start
writing poetry
while she was still alive
She would have liked that
We could have steered
clear of her wounds and built
another fine bridge between us

Mother, you are this living thing
a circle embracing us

Your grandchildren remember you
spending evenings in a beige
corduroy armchair, book in hand
too engrossed in it to notice
the closing of the door

Twenty five years since your passing
I have stepped in your steps—
more precisely, I'm now sitting in your place
in my own quilted leather armchair
its sienna a tad darker

My back bends in your curve
the left elbow kneads the armrest
the right cradles a book
ready to turn the page
honoring the closing of the circle

WHAT BAKA SAID

*Life is good
when there is enough time to read.*

She often fell asleep with glasses on.
Her book slid on a feather duvet
she stitched in three-inch squares
so the feathers wouldn't shift.

She was a mistress of intricacies
like lining the bedding buttons twice
for extra softness.

There was more wisdom and love
in matching those buttons
than could be packed into a crate of books.

At night she would get in bed
with a favorite novel.
The first thing in the morning, she made sure
the bookmark was still in place—
her daily activities, mere interruptions
between chapters.

I'm nearing the end
she would say and add with a chuckle
*Of the book
Can you take me to the library?*

Usually the only customer
in the foreign language section
her silvery hair went well
with the dust jackets of used books.

When she died she left me three things:

Her beloved book collection in Croatian—
read and reread; it reclined between
a pair of jasper rook bookends
the other chess pieces long missing
perhaps mixed in with the children's toys.

Some frayed and yellowed pages
written in an old-person's cursive—
a translation of her recipes
from Croatian to English
the back-bone of my cuisine.

A night table cover
handmade in a traditional
red and black zigzag motif

now a doily for the book of fairy tales
I read as a child
when she was just my mother
and not yet a Baka.

LIVING IN A BUTTERFLY WORLD

Silvery and auburn hair
mingled confidentially

My mother thought the butterflies
more beautiful in her youth:

How they fluttered on the lawn
sprinkling pure joy

paraded those shapely wings
of unimaginable colors

All was motion, all was dance
Tiny dervishes of dust

whirled in sunbeams
as she stood alone

mesmerized
oblivious to time

A sudden tolling of
the school bell broke the spell

Any minute now, and with a clang
the heavy door will shut itself

The staccato sound
of running

kept tempo
with her pounding heart

She must be on time!
She must pay respects

to the bar of steel
that scrapes

the mud off the shoes
leaves outdoors behind

She must keep
that classroom clean

in which none
believed her stories

and nobody ever wept
for beauty of butterflies

Coming home alone, her tears
tasted of disappointment

Then she opened windows
and waited for butterflies

BAKA'S HOUR

When I entered her room
she lifted her eyes
full of the story in her book

remembered it was time
for her evening ice cream
and turned the right hand palm up
like a child about to receive a gift.

Life has handed her more than a fair
share of hardships and heartbreaks—
still, she smiled at me every evening
of her old age, a happy woman.

Sometimes I sent my children
to bring her ice cream:
It was important that they see
her face light up.

They still call her Baka.
The aroma of her pastries
the home-made apple strudel
and the cheese *kiflice*
has never left the house.

When I make the same
they call them Baka's goodies
almost as good as hers.

This is how the children connect
to what is important in life.
I encourage them
as I slide into her role.

BAKA ON AN ESCALATOR

She came from somewhere else
and didn't know of moving stairs
on which the way one feels
is neither up nor down.

In an old-fashioned dress of limpid brown
she tried hard to retain poise
while the stairs kept seeping away
like miles of disappearing sand.

How to venture a first step
when one is from somewhere else?
How to replace one's place?

When she was young
she relished shinning trees
the taller the better
but none floated on air.

She paused, regrouped
took the first step
because the escalator belt
hummed in her granddaughter's voice:

Baka, you can make it.
You can make it.

RAINY DAY CONCERTS
for Božidar, my father

The rainy days and concerts
descended seasonally
a steady overture of raindrops
playing on the windowpane.

The kitchen was small:
A table and stove
and my father standing tall
without an instrument.

On a low step-stool
my friend and I, his audience
begged for a performance.

He blew air through his cheeks
clearing his throat for a special effect
and launched the sounds of a trumpet
the high notes through his right cheek
the bass through his left.

The kitchen became a concert hall.

He loved his rituals
shaved for the occasion:
Smooth cheeks make smooth sounds.

I believed him.
He let me poke his cheeks, pretending
I was the one who made the music.

He nodded, I turned the pages
of the music which he didn't need.
He enjoyed engaging his audience.

He let us choose a melody
from a repertoire of operas
the vestiges of that other life
of gentility.

Wistful notes crept in from
the young man he used to be—
a master of music and his life.

When his face turned crimson
my mother intervened
Oh Božo, you don't want to overdo it.

Some seventy years later
the warm finger of a toddler
pokes my laughing cheek.

I see the face of my father
feel his smooth shaven skin
warm under my fingertip.

Love in reprise.

ARTIFACT

I watched my mother
tie a cravat for my father
and tighten it just so
tenderness
in the angle of her head.

He stood tall, she petite.
She'd lift her arms up to him—
standing on her toes
the waves of her luxuriant black hair
couldn't reach up to his chin.

She'd hand him his attache case
hold the door, give him a smile
to last him the whole day, like you see
in those classic movies of the Fifties.

She headed to the kitchen.
He to his job in Old Town.

My father used to walk with
a cane that hardly touched the ground—
the affectation of a prewar dandy.

Carved on the cane's handle
a shaggy black dog pricked up his ears
trying to catch a phrase.

Is this your father, Mirna?
So handsome, walking with a cane
such a gentleman.

How proud I was then, before
the sounds of war and ugly
arguments choked my happiness.

The walking cane became an artifact
of the past thrown away
wrapped carefully in crumpled newspaper

The dog's ears still alert, listening
the news no longer relevant.

II.
THE BELOVED GHOSTS

To see the truth
one must step back pretty far

THEN, WHAT IS TRUE

Some members
of my maternal family gallery
remain ghosts

images that fail to emerge
from developing liquid
of a darkroom

There are more question marks
than answers
in their life story

the sparse details true
as far as I know

ETUŠ | ESTERA
my mother's younger sister

Were you a part
of a naked agonizing mass
flailing limbs
gasps, screams

a scene from *Inferno*
beyond what Dante could imagine?

What were the sins
of those condemned
to this hell without flames?

The gas hissed:
Birth-sins
Birth-sins
HISSSSSS

At the end, the shock of death
without dignity
piles of bodies
caked with lime
topped with clumps of earth

Which clump are you now?

When from the comfort
of my plush seat
in a movie theater
I saw heaps of bodies on the silver screen
I don't want to believe I saw you

Your name left no trace:
The German archives opened
only to the German-born

It was the law that
left no space for shadows

Three quarters of a century later
the archives opened up—

your name and death
starkly on the page—
a black crime on white
the bare facts without
the grisly particulars

It WAS Auschwitz
where the trains came
to a dead end
All dead

The rest of your story
will be left forever
to cold conjecture

ROZA | RUŽA
my mother's older sister

A resistance fighter
a Jew

A warrant was out for her
A double prize

A sweet lady with
a soft white neck
nobody could save

The Nazis shot you
hanged you like a puppet
from the flagpole in front of
the School of Pedagogy in Aleksinac

Where you taught the youngsters
how to become teachers
with an emphasis on
what is right and what is wrong

Your limp, dangling body
an example

IZO | IZRAEL
my mother's younger brother

Thirty-four years
of your young life

compressed into three lines
of the concentration camp archives

Sandberg, Izrael, a Jew
murdered by the Ustaše
in Jasenovac, in 1942

Izo, I don't remember you at all
I miss not knowing more about you
It's too late for that
Forgive me

MARCI | MARTIN
my mother's older brother

Marci
lithe and strong

The brother
who climbed trees

With my mother
a tomboy

Marci
who always won

The boyish games
but lost the game of life

Before he had a chance

FANI | FRANCIKA
Marci's wife

The same first name
as my mother Fani Križnić
whose diacritics saved her life

Fani Sandberg could have been
a proper German name
but not when it's paired
with curly black hair
shorn at induction

Inside the barbed wire
lips blistered on empty cups
fists held on to crumbs

Sleep when it came
heavy from exhaustion
light from listening
    for barking orders
    the thud of riffle butts
    a crackling of shots

A nightmare
day and night

Dead in a year

ACO | ARMIN
the older son of Marci and Fani

At an angle to comfort, an angel
leans towards me protectively

He wore a mariner suit
navy with white

Had a congenital hip defect
It happens

My Omama said
God was even-handed
when he endowed Aco
with great intelligence
but a faulty gait

A bright ten-year old
limping to his death

Oh, Aco, my gangly cousin!
When I saw you last

your long arms
hugged my narrow shoulders

Then they took you away

Made you stop growing
in less than six months

MARKICA | MARKO
the younger son of Marci and Fani

No record of you in Jasenovac—
Too young to survive the arrival

A two-year old
a cuddly toy
the family darling

in a light pantsuit
three mother-of-pearl buttons
hair shiny brown, parted to the side
face round, wide black eyes

Am I remembering you
or your photograph?

Having been three years old
my memory is a trickster

LINA AND JOSEF | JOSIP SANDBERG

My grandparents
Omama and Otata
rescued from a train
bound for the camps of death

By someone
they never learned who

It could have been
a German officer
lodging in their tiny room

who in his great craving
looked into the wrinkles
on the face of my Omama
and thought
he recognized his mother

Afterwards she used to say
reaching for the corner of her apron

I wish
he saved my children instead
If it was he

III.
EYES OF SILENCE

Ask the red poppies—
they come back every year
but the dead do not

EYES OF SILENCE

What happened
to my decimated family
I'll never know

Eyelids sting red hot
conscience burns white cold

My mouth sealed by the
silence of others and my own

Should I have inquired more
poked the raw wounds
of the dear ones
who survived?

♦ ♦ ♦

Sorrow billows in my steps
tapping for the threads
that bound our lives together

and however brief and fragile
our braided, shortened paths
our love living in my breath
watches over me like an angel

SANCTUARY

I keep sorrow
in a sanctuary
reserved for beauty

All kinds of beauty—
radiant smiles
gentle words
creamy camellias
infinite waves of sand dunes

In that haven
they hold hands together

There my sorrow reveals
a face of love

MY OMAMA

Her shirred, earth-brown
dress grew tiny flowers
in each step

Apron solid black—
two large pockets
to hold the trinkets
waiting to be put
back in place

Also for surprises

Slippers
gray, thick felt
Shiny buttons
on each side
tightened
with elastic bands
tough enough to stretch

Smooth gray hair
pulled into a bun

Teary green eyes
kindly smile
a beauty in her youth

I didn't know this
She was my Omama

DUMPLINGS AND PARSNIP ROOT

Omama bestowed on me her love
apricot dumplings, fresh cottage cheese
and sour cream, scarce after the war.

She'd scoop me up over the threshold
called me *my Miniuška* and notice
how much I'd grown since our last visit.

Otata was lying ill in the room
no point in calling it a bedroom—there was
no other room except for a kitchen.

At night, my mother and I snuggled up
to the tall Delft-tiled stove
like two overgrown cats

while Omama ministered
tea and sympathy
to her husband wasting away.

On better days they'd let me see him—
the flowers stenciled on the opaque walls
fresh and cheerful as if summers never end
all inclined in the same angle.

I bent down to kiss him.
He gave me a skewed smile
feebly moving his hands closer to mine.

I asked: *Is he any better?*
They shooed me out
Your Otata . . . he needs rest.

In the end
I never got to know him very well.

These visits weren't sad for me
I didn't know how much I'd be missing him
and I loved my Omama dearly.

I loved the way she feigned surprise
when I untied her apron
and the way she carried burning pots
with bare hands, made soups
whose vapors refused to evaporate.

I heard my mother and Omama
To make a good chicken soup you need
chicken wings and chicken feet
celery and carrots
parsley and parsnip root

Omama didn't talk about her losses.
Tears trickled down her face sparsely.
Old people probably run out of them.

They spoke of many things, skirted more.
I didn't comprehend those late night talks.
Later, afraid of what they meant
I didn't dare ask.

Years passed. Lives ended.
The questions went unattended.
Now I have no one to ask.

SACKS OF TAWNY WALNUTS
for my uncle Vlado

From the bank of a mighty river
I'm watching a boat drift away
a white sail turn into a butterfly
at the end of the rolling river.
    Will it come back to me?
    Will it ever?

On the day he returned
to his ancestral home
Vlado sang that song for me
until I knew it by heart
as we bounced merrily
on a four-poster bed.

I was a child. He acted like one.

He looted the cellar
for the tawny walnuts in sacks
tied with hemp, with care.
I stood sentry for the sound of slippers
and the silhouette of my grandmother.

He scattered the walnuts in forgotten places
for me to uncover later.

We retied the sacks with whispers and giggles.
I promised to remember the song.
We said our goodbyes.
He closed the door and left
to fight in the resistance war.

The last time he came, his mother told him:
My son, don't come back
sinister men are stalking this house.
You are endangering yourself
and your ancestral home.

He never came back at all
from the rivers and forests of war.
I waited for him, sang his song
under the walnut tree, alone.

ROOTS OF CAUTION

The summer is here
Time to eat corn
mow the sweet cobs
steadily from left to right
as if nibbling on a toy harmonica

My uncle Vlado
used to play it like a virtuoso
He pretended he was a warbler
and declared birds
more musical than humans

I wondered about that for years
He also promised to buy me a real
harmonica with shiny tin sides flashing
and a mouth-board smelling of pine

Then he left to fight in the War
and never returned
so I couldn't hold him to it

Better not to promise
even when it's out of love

POPPIES IN THE FALLOW FIELDS

After the War the fields went fallow—

no wheat, only poppies
crimson from the blood of fallen heroes

I used to pick them
before I knew my uncle was one of them

WITNESSING THE VOID

Not a cloth
A hole in the cloth

A rip
Not a seam

A chair
I didn't want to tuck in

For fear of making
hopelessness permanent

I witnessed the void

BOMBING FLARES

We rushed outside
to watch the flares drop
from the blameless sky

although we knew
nothing good would
come out of it

Once in a while
a brilliant cluster of light flashed

spilling a treacherous glow
over targets

The children exclaimed: *WOW!*

The grownups said
stern and horrified
hush, children, hush
dragging us inside

They called them
Christmas lights

breathtaking
even as they took away
the breath from the unlucky ones

IV.
C IS FOR CAMELLIA

The bees might be busy knitting
a yellow lace in the flower-cradles

C IS FOR CAMELLIA

Mother held a squirming child
high up to a blooming tree

pudgy legs around
her curvy hips

Be still, my pretty girly-girl

She moved a stray curl
away from her daughter's face

The bees might be busy knitting
a yellow lace in the flower-cradles

She scanned it twice
let her smell it up close

until her little nose became
a golden buttercup

They both laughed
the same merry laugh

A small brook of joy
gurgled and wouldn't stop

Tonight when the moon is high
I'll sing you a lullaby

I'll cover you with creamy petals
and caress your camellia fingers

until you float on a camellia dream
Sia mia camelia

NINA NANA
for Violet

I said to my Violet:
*What will you name
your dolly?*

I won't name her

*Then what will you
call your dolly?*

*She is Dolly
and that's what
I will call her*

She laid her
in the middle
of a swinging bench

lined with fabric
of bright daisies
bluebells and violets

covered her with
a favorite blanket
tucked her in tenderly and said:

*You stay in the middle, Dolly
not close to the edge
'cause you might fall, Dolly*

and that would
give you an owie, Dolly
and owies hurt

She sang to her "Nina nana"
the same "Nina nana"
that her Mommy sings to her

and said to herself:
Now I am your Mommy

TEMPORARY BLISS
for Audrey

Little Audrey came
to sit in my lap

Her small wriggly weight
a gift

wrapped in restless layers
of silky tissue paper

A fresh scent of
her recently washed hair

wafted through the air
We just sat together

After a while I asked her:
Would you like to play a game?

She glanced at her toys
tilted her head and said:

Let's stay here like this

SCHERZO
for Elena

Not much
is ever said
about elbows
as such

but when they nudge
the ribs of a sibling
with a pokey touch

angels giggle

PLAYING HOOKY

I wasn't the kind of kid
who plays hooky

I loved school—
the smell of paper, perfume
the scribble of a pencil, a possibility

School loved me back
as a wall loves a coat-hook
as the school bell loves
the whoosh-whoosh of small feet
gliding over the red maple leaves

That day, the sun shone
on the cover of a travel magazine
sending shivers
from my feet to my collar bone

For the sake of excitement
I left through the window
my classmates busy spreading
the newest gossip

No one noticed

Grownups owned the streets
I owned time and loneliness

I moseyed around
watched the wind play
with a small piece of trash
lodge it at the mouth of
the cast iron sewer grate
which refused to swallow it

The morning wasn't fit to spin
an awesome fable about it:

No parades on weekdays
no oompah or recorded music
oozing from the stores

only the customers
in subdued clothing
mostly without packages
looking exasperated

A shrill voice cut
through the crowd:
Hey, kid, why aren't you in school?

I asked myself the same question
The adventure disappointed
I felt for the coins in my pocket
wishing for the tram, Red, Number Eight
the round trip, the last hurrah

I returned the way I came
through the window, during recess
Scraped a knee

No one noticed

The Red tram, Number Eight
almost forgotten

What a day it wasn't!

MEMENTO

I opened an old book
out fell a summer day

A breeze kissed the face
of Old Woman Lake
blew dry leaves from her hips
all over her splendid belly

They tickled
she giggled
ruffled her quiet surface
and called for a regatta

The leaves circled, whirled
until they came ashore
tripped over each other
making a fluffy nest
out of the school playground

The children made a sport of them
piled them into sliding heaps, played
the houses-for-bugs with them
then brought some home and
pressed them in the books

I know this. I was there
A dry leaf in my hands

BRIDGING AN ARROYO

Why tell you things
about myself?
You are a stranger

I wanted to call a friend
but an arroyo between us
stayed my hand

and the clouds
wafting in the sky
didn't bring the rain

I wanted to write a letter
but the white sheet froze
and remained pristine

Yesterday
the gray car whizzed by
without stopping for me

Now you know
You are no longer
a stranger

THE THIRD PASSENGER

He drives along
an irrelevant road

She reaches out
caresses his hair

once curly, black
now a silvery fluff

Eyes on the road
his face barely turned

A gratified smile
emerges in silence

Men don't say much
about their feelings

The caressing fingers
whisper: *I like the feel*

of your mane, my lion
Women say more!

The glow of his smile
lights up her face

Love rides along
an irrelevant road

SIMPLY SAID, *AMARCORD*
(*I remember* in Romagnolo dialect)

Tonino Guerra, a master poet
of simple and genuine
the author of the script
for Fellini's *Amarcord*

told how his father upon
Tonino's return from war
stood on the threshold
and in the way of greeting
and kissing him, asked:
    Have you eaten yet?

I recalled my Omama
standing in front of her threshold

Gathered layers of her skirt
fluttered in the breeze
the pale sun on her right
plated her hair-bun
with late afternoon light

She swept me up, kissed me
embraced my mother and asked:
    Have you eaten yet?

A thousand miles between
the two lands, a canyon of
unrelated languages

asking the same unadorned question

WAITING FOR THE LIGHT

My muse, a gypsy heart
who reserves the right
to change her mind

Akhmatova
you whose Tartar blood
brews exuberance
come and laugh

Call this silence a pause
a whim in a dark blue night
Visit me tomorrow—

Shafts of light will dance
the Boogie-Woogie
on the grass

V.
GALLERY OF PORTRAITS

They sussurate
I listen

I HAVE A BIRD FRIEND
for Jane Kos

She understands my chatter
the garbled sounds

I learned to make
before I left my native tree

It is not a chatter she was
born into, but at one time

she visited the same tree long
enough to feel its purling beauty

Now the two of us delight
in smoothing the bird-vowels

and strolling over the consonants
whose clusters of twos or threes

gurgle like brook water
splashing over pebbles

When I share with her the route
I travelled every scented summer

through the pine forest in Rovinj
on the way to the open beach

she knows what I mean
She also understands

the word *simpatica* and
together we get carried away

in a prattle-gabble jibber-jabber
and that makes her dear to me

TONY

Houses borrow the personality of the owner.
This one, boisterous with
doors swung wide open, inviting.

Fragrant roses spill out
of the chipped terra-cotta pots.

On the porch brushed by the sinking sun
the old man rescues stories from
the abyss of World War One
not at all in tune with history
which the youngsters don't learn anyway
and the elderly, like him, forget.

An aura of time, like silver polish
absolves him of prejudice and
a certain steeliness of eye dissolves
into a smile of a harmless, amicable
man offering a version of himself
to anyone passing by.

Other times, he rode his wheelchair
deliberately on busy roads
slowing down the runaway world
claiming to be in command.

Summer at an end
a stranger is watering his lawn.
No Tony in sight.
Was the heat too much for him?

I miss his wheelchair
his grins and lack of delicacy
his loud remarks
trying to persuade the world
he's still kicking.
And I miss him.

I search the facade of his silent house
fear mounting in my throat
a foreboding becoming
a certainty.

On the mossy roof, the tiles nestle
same as always
although nothing is ever the same.

A LILAC WORLD
for Nada (Hope)

I lived in my no-sister and
no-brother childhood.
It was spring: The air full of promise
and vague hopes.

I wandered around looking for a friend.
A pair of golden-wheat braids in
a blue polka-dotted dress
peeked around the corner
of a stuccoed house.

She said: *Would you like to play with me?*
and I said: *Oh, yes.*

We played together that day and the next
until we grew up.
She had two brothers but she wanted a sister.

I loved her house of lilac branches
which leaned on the window panes
trying to look inside.

I loved the old apple tree whose petals
felt like restless feathers
on our outstretched hands.

We danced with them a weightless dance
such as only children can—
clumsy, graceful
serious and playful.

The flower pots full of soil
watched and waited for us
to begin the planting games.

Afterwards, my friend's mother scolded her
for staining her only dress
but being polite, she never scolded a guest.

Before darkness descended
I carried the scent of lilac back
to my no-sister and no-brother world.

When my mother scolded me
for staining my only dress
I felt closer to my friend.

I couldn't wait for tomorrow.

MRS. KÖNIG WOULD HAVE BEEN A HUNDRED AND FIFTY YEARS OLD TODAY

She was *Die Königin*, The Queen.

A natural queen.
Gauzy loom-spun clothes in earth colors
looked dignified on her.

The Queen of Candles
that don't melt or bend
but become more luminous.

The Queen of her house.
She ruled without ruling. Her way was love.

She mourned her long lost husband
plunged her hands into the fertile garden soil
saying: *He would've approved of that.*

The town people thought her pixilated;
still, they came around, offered help.
*No, thank you, but I could provide
for the homeless plants.*

Her legendary garden crossed
the borders into the surreal.

My grandmother, the only visitor
brought her home-baked goodies—
they both preferred giving and receiving.

She asked what was my favorite flower
took me by the hand, walked up to
a larkspur, *genus delphinium*.

The flower I meant was larger.

She said: *Look for beauty in small things.*
Mother nature knows best. If it wanted
to make a large flower, it would've done that.
The cultivated flowers are only ALSO beautiful.

It was a glorious garden: Wild flowers
thrived with their hybrid relatives.

She could've taught botany at any university
but nobody thought to invite her.
She would have declined anyway.

The botany taught in my school was
annually and perennially disappointing
the lessons devoid of her magic which
I found later in my own garden.

When I planted delphiniums
they winked at me and summoned
her unwrinkled apparition
wearing a nature-lover's smile.

Mrs. König never died—
she escaped into a whimsy
of her flowers and butterflies
and chose not to return.

On some early mornings
I hear her voice:

So ... you like delphiniums?
A pause, a big breath ... May I tell you ...

THE LAST TIME I SAW MY FRIEND
for Sonja

A few strands of silvery hair
escaped from a gauzy cap
barely hiding an ugly scar
underneath the wrap.

She calmly told me she was treated well.
The nurses liked her—
there was no point in making a fuss.
Her weak bird-hands fluttered over mine
trying to console me.

They came for her to take more tests.
We said what could be said, embraced
said sweet parting words.

She shuffled through the lounge, turned around
and looked at me for the last time
with feverish El Greco eyes.

Hope between the lacquered swinging door
and the opaque wall, receded into a black line.

She was gone.

I flew home that night—
she passed away while I was in the sky.

I grieved. Emailed a poem.
Her granddaughter rewrote it
in solemn cursive
placed a note without an envelope
on top of the wooden coffin.

The granddaughter went on with her life
I went on with mine. We lost touch.

I wish I asked her for a sample
of her writing, so I could imagine
our friendship resting on the bed of
white roses and creamy chrysanthemums.

FRAU ELSA

On the fifth of February, I received the news:
A classmate had suddenly died
and on Monday was her funeral.

I used to walk to school with her for years
because no one else lived close to my house—
I didn't know yet I craved to visit her grandmother.

Frau Elsa was thin of limb and quite tall
wrapped in a foreign-looking shawl
an old Austrian dame
brimming with high culture and sensitivity

much too fine for her tobacco-store-owner
husband who entertained the customers
by telling them his wife was too nervous for
an ordinary life, the one he could offer her.

He never forgave her the dowry
which bought him the store.
They felt for him, watched her fragile form
squirm in smoky clouds of nicotine.

She'd hand me a lollipop—her kindness
soothing like her wrinkled hands.
Once I tried to tell her that I loved her.
I don't think she heard me through the din
or perhaps I never uttered it.

Instead, I played with my friend
whose sturdy father and
jolly, solicitous mother
hovered over a new pressboard table
too well varnished to be played on:
I missed my old wooden one
marked with many doodles.

Living on another continent
for fifty years I didn't think about
our two tables or my ill-matched friend.

When I heard the news
a small fiber within me snapped
leaving a resonance of my childhood.

I went to sleep that night
grieving for Frau Elsa's trembling hands.

A CONFESSION AT 3 AM

A little house

curled up

under a roof of sleeping slate

granting me the solitude

of quiet hours

The sprites visit

bringing gifts:

A half-finished poem

a fragrant peach

a handful of red mulberries

in a basket woven

with pine sap

and a thought

of you and me

Although the two of us

never happened

it was the sweetest dream

VI.
LANDSCAPES OF THE HEART

Cream of old lace
sienna of worn brocade

THE PIAZZA

In a Fellini movie
the stardust of wonderment
blends the piazza on the screen
with the one in my heart

Perhaps I was born in this place
or I lived here once
in a previous life, if I had one
or I just dreamt it

The piazza is sunbaked and pale
cream of old lace
sienna of worn brocade

A delicate green of young hyacinths
sprouts in majolica planters

I recognize the noises
The clatter of carts rolling
down uneven cobblestones
The cats meowing plaintively

The daily exchanges
in Mediterranean households
bravado hanging in the air

Someone scolds a child
someone else a spouse—
the sounds of *my* and *mine*

*My dear God, my Madonna
my children, my worries—*

I'm in love with this place
that remembers both
what did exist and what didn't

People have lived here since
the first village recorded
in the town archives

of musty books on shelves
and the maps
hung on the walls
like dried bats

An old man on a rickety chair
draws circles in the dust
with a worn-out cane

He taps his memory, tells stories
about his grandfathers and uncles
who wore their eccentricity
on their sleeve

In those days
the houses honored furniture—
this piece brought by Elda
a blushing bride
that one carved by Peppino
a neighbor's son
in the year of the great drought

Possessions, dignified, not luxurious
used to have a history

The old man falls asleep
his chin resting on his chest

The piazza waits for me
a faded star in the sea of cobblestone
streets spread like arms I long for

How long will it take...

HAMLET IN DUBROVNIK

I didn't count how many steps
to see Hamlet

I was a teenager
one in a crowd
climbing the shoulders
of old Fort Lovrijenac
a Mediterranean Elsinore

The lush green of conifers
blocked the view
of the black-blue sea below
scenting the air
with night-incense

Musky torches flickered
setting the mood
until the play started
our voices in a reverent hush

On the brink of the old bastion
loomed the ghost of the Father
shrouded in white, an ominous spirit
revealing the skeleton of crime

At the feet of deaf walls
the sea pounded a watery complaint
upon indignant cliffs
unmoved as if they never heard of murder
in life or a story

Waves and stanzas
stars low on the horizon
brilliantine and the sultry odor of the sea

Sixty years later, back in Dubrovnik
I search my bones for memories
squinting in the glaring daylight
scanning the hills for the familiar
contour of the fort

The blue patches of sea
frolic with green stripes of cypress trees
Matisse cutouts
drunk with summer heat

A hundred and seventy-two steps
too steep for my aching knees
swollen in the humid breeze
pungent with evergreen and laurel

The light begins to dim
I reach the plateau of split travertine—
one half the stage
the other for the audience

I caress the warm railing
close my eyes
and wait for the specter of my youth
to walk the parapet above the sea

UNDECIPHERED IN CAPUA

Eternal Astarte makes her morning rounds
wakes buds, warms bird nests
lends life to the statues of *Mater Matutae*—

The Mothers of Dawn
carved in porous Campanian tuff
among doves, pomegranates
and remnants of ancient Oscan script

Worn by rain and wind
features corroded, details gone
the Mothers dressed in tunics
embrace ten or more
swaddled babies in each ample lap

Elbows inclined in a mute chant of stone
they swing their burdens gently
in a tender fashion of primitive
never-changing motherhood

Thus I remember the sleepy town of Capua
left to the mercy of the blazing sun:

Tight-lipped shutters, an echo
of footsteps telling stories to
the dust devils that whirl in deserted streets

And not a soul outside to guide you
to a lost museum where the Mater Matutae
live silent, stoney-still, and undeciphered

CANTO OF AN OLEANDER BUD

On an abandoned quay
the pink oleander blossoms

dropped delicate veils
over a late summer day

The vacation ended
all good things in life too short

Unpalpable new longings
stirred like hopeful grass

From the vault of miracles
out of sync with my melancholy

the North Star twinkled
promising delight

I heard footfalls behind me
felt delicate touch

on my braided hair
an oleander bud

A gift of the moment
impossible to hold—

a wisp of something
dividing the remaining days into

the oleander ones
and all the others

PAINTED NAILS

I met a friend on Punta Corrente
where rosy oleander shrubs
wove frilly garlands around
the knobby knees of stately pines

Oleanders that thrive there still
may be the same ones
or the offspring of underbrush
it's hard to tell

Time in those parts stands still
and nature doesn't cater
to the trespassers

We snapped the leaves off the twigs
to paint our nails with their oozing tears

When they dried
the pink lacquered petals
gleamed on our adolescent fingers

What delightful frivolity
I never knew such extravagance

Huddled under the tree-crowns
we whispered grave girlish secrets
like two budding witches plotting
pranks on gullible men

Then one day she didn't come
Curtains drawn on her vacant house

On the front steps
empty bottles rolled back and forth
In the corners, busy spiders spun
filmy webs over peeling paint

I kept returning like a swell
searching for the magic scent
of days of oleander
with a hint of pine

I never found it

The oleander sap
the glue of our summer friendship
dried up long ago

WAKE UP CALL

A tranquil lake
surrounded by sleeping pines

slumbering shadows
on a glassy mirror

No line between reality and dreams
disturbed the calm

A duckling tried to fly
Her webbed feet inscribed

a shimmering arrow
over filmy water

The lake shivered
bartered

its gray gown of lead
for a pure silver crepe

The duckling was flying low
and aimlessly

unaware of the magic
of her wake up call

Her keen eyes caught
a flicker in the water

She dove in
concentric circles behind her

A chatter of sundry birds
shattered the silence

Slender grasses stirred
Willows knee-deep in the lake

shook the dew off
their silky leaves

whispered
good morning

BEACH MINUET

Pebbles baking in the summer day

Out to see the sunset
the barefoot boys and girls
skip gingerly around them

Nervous turnbulls, eager seagulls
and elegant egrets tiptoe
in a delicate minuet

Pelicans observe

Sun-globe sinks into the ocean's well
Sparkling rubies ride the waves
the last joy-ride of the day

Mesmerized, the spectators
linger with the sun
then they too are gone

The birds fly away
The hot pebbles exhale
the last breath of the day

Dusk descends on an empty beach

Not a soul stirs, not a hair—
shh, shh, shushes drowsy air
Let the beach sleep

VII.
THE WAYWARD LOGIC OF DREAMS

River flowing up the hills
hills learning to swim

TIEPOLO SKY

I craved to see a Tiepolo sky
blue with a blush of peach

oh so vast
one could evaporate

vanish into space
and no one would notice

I stepped onto the balcony—
no clouds to anchor my gaze

no need to orient myself in space
From the corner of my eye

two white specks appeared
grew wings and elongated

necks with peach colored beaks
turning into elegant white ibises

With each passing moment
more sublime

the sky filled
with soft shiny feathers

silence
bliss

THE WAYWARD LOGIC OF DREAMS

Between wakefulness and sleep

a line surreal, so fine
it reposes in reverie

What a dream I had!
Rules off, boundaries adrift

rivers flowing up the hills
hills learning to swim

humans grow angelic wings
birds with human feet

dance a jig
and there's more:

The moon waltzes out at 10 am
the sun at midnight at its best

Such a world knows only happiness
All is here for the taking

slumber through the day
sow wheat under starlight

the crop ready, François Millet has
painted a new version of *Haystacks*

Nocturnal animals alter their appetites
knock on my door at noon, polite

waiting for the meal to be served
on shells of gleaming abalone

What a lovely life-design
Fruit falling into our hands

But my heart isn't buying it
Where are the travails, the sorrows

the satisfaction of effort
the hope and waiting

Where's the thrill
of anticipation?

Achievement and its reward
asleep

Listen to the sheep
baah, baah

in a continuous orgy
of contentment

A dream fit for
deep sleep

Don't you agree?

FELLINI-ESQUE

The sun, playing with pastels
drew a rosy sunset over Tuscan hills.

In the middle of an undulating road
an enormous turkey opened his enormous wings.
A crimson rose sprung from his heart.

He wouldn't move. A line of cars
stopped abruptly raising dust
veiling all but the bird in
a dreamy haze.

The turkey was beautiful
in black, brown and white feathers
like a cosmatesque mosaic
on a medieval church floor.

The red rose shook
moved to a proper place on his crest
and a mute procession commenced.

In a theatrical motion, the turkey pulled
a sign PEOPLE CROSSING out of his wing
planted it on the left bank of the road
and a large THANK YOU sign, on the right.

Other animals appeared out of nowhere:
A couple of sheep, woolly and beige
a shiny-tailed rooster with a speckled hen
two bearded goats, and two giraffes
in rust-colored, white-spotted blazers
all on their way to Noah's Ark.

Astonished crowds watched the spectacle:
The big turkey enjoyed playing crossing guard—
he swung his flexible wing-batons with relish
nudged lovingly the slower-moving animals
and pecked a little at the dawdling ducklings.

He winked discreetly to his audience
raised the THANK YOU sign very high
folded his wings over his breast
and bowed ceremoniously.

Then Chaplin-like, he tipped his crest to us
and slid into the sunset
that swallowed all colors
except the crimson of the rose
which lingered until a gray hand
gently but finally, swept the scene away.

Waking up in a hot Madrid hotel room—
Why dream of Tuscan hills in Spain
a turkey on a mosaic floor
and ducks?

Ah yes, the children's book
Make Way for Ducklings
How the spirits of the night play
peek-a-boo with the events of the day!

In the lull of the nascent morning
a faint-crested voice:

Love and dreams
Leave them be
lest they lose their charm.

SUNSET

A weary, old work horse
out to breathe the dust of excitement
by trotting and galloping

wanted to be a part of
the general commotion
of a proper horse race.

He didn't have the means or the manners
only the desire.
His owner not responding to his pleading looks
he neighed to his fellow horses
who were indignant and incredulous.

Then he whinnied to some old cronies who were
in horse's terms, prone to taking risks
and finally neighed them into bolting.

All at once they felt exhilarated.
No racing tracks for them—only
the plushest clover-covered meadow
the one sprawling by the farm house
stretching out as far as the eye can see.

They knew every plant in it
every indentation of the soil.

They raced and raced in balmy evening breeze
until the meadow trembled under their speed
and the clover leaves bowed in trepidation.

Our horse won.
He received a prancing ovation.
The farm boys and girls came out
to witness this incredible parade and
the owner's son gave him a cube of sugar
and spoke to him in admiration.

Tired after such a feat
he trotted slowly through his own sunset.

On the way to the stables
he held his head higher than usual.
His nostrils opened wider to inhale
the joy that lingered in the scent of
the freshly trampled grass.

His hoof caught in the hole
a diligent mole burrowed last night
he stumbled genuflecting unintentionally.

Going down, he beheld
the meadow of his first and last race.

ELVES OF HOPE

Last night I dreamt of my death

Nobody around me:
No husband, children, friends
only the caretakers
at their austere work

I craved to see dear faces
bending over mine
instead of a flock of crows
crowding one another
pecking at my china

Shoo, birds, plunder some place else—
take your bickering ways with you
leave me to the elves of hope

The sheets feel clammy
though made of the softest cotton
How can I feel anything at all?

My eyelashes made of lead
I flounder in the dark
groping for the shower
to cool my feverish skin

Let the day begin
with pearly drops of water

Let the morning dew
wash away the nightmare
and replace it with trivia

I'm not so choosy anymore
anything simple will do:
Some dry clothes and slippers

especially the slippers
the comfortable toes
wiggling happily in plushy padding

and the familiar groan
of the loose floor board
as I amble by

ON THE ROAD TO BANFF

Uncovered by early morning sun
the mountain peaks showed up reluctantly

Their shoulders, ancient swords
in a tournament of contrasts
pared light with flinty edges
as sharp as steel blades

Thus Mount Rundle stood
exposed, ogled, photographed
to be owned by foolish people
in the privacy of their home

or publicly on a large screen
flattened and impoverished
reduced to fit the human taste
for the spectacular

A camera-shutter click
a shudder of an insect's wing
a tiny icon, an image, a mere souvenir—
how are they related
to the immovable mountain?

The splendid original perseveres
impervious to rain and fog
lightning and fire
indifferent to the pleading
of its own eroding skin

and to all but time
measured in eons

ENTRANCED

Lights dim at Lincoln Center

Melodies swell
dance on waves

Honey-colored velvet curtain
parts like liquid gold

Ethereal nymphs shimmer
pirouette on satiny points
hummingbirds
too fast for a human eye

❖ ❖ ❖

Ballerina unravels the cotton
wound around her wounded toes
reminding her she was a burst of beauty
a butterfly perched
in an arabesque

❖ ❖ ❖

Driving home through darkness
a couple watches headlights dance
they don't want the charm to end

IN THE LEOPOLD MUSEUM IN VIENNA

The way people talk about Gustav Klimt
one would think he invented the kiss
He didn't
Millions of lovers never heard of him

Nor did he invent square frames
He did use them in novel ways
to contain the lushness of his trees

The trees escape
and inhabit the spacious museum
looking for an open window
Finding none, they lodge in your eyes

Nothing's left except you
in a world of green

And those leaves—
how they breathe, draw you in
lift you up until you levitate

the trees inhabiting
the chambers of your mind and heart

joy blossoming
in your hands

Now imagine
the flights of fancy
of their creator
Gustav Klimt

Do
I dare you!

MOONSTONES AND A BIRD

I hear you, my unborn children
through the malachite
of a wakeful night—

my brooding thoughts
opaque moonstones
still the secrets of the Deep

❖ ❖ ❖

Morning finds the bird
huddled on a wire
not ready to sing

She burrows her head in
a feathery wing

The wire vibrates
heart palpitates

She resonates and waits
for the notes to come
the light too shy to arrive

and deliver
the moonstones
from the depth of
the malachite sea

VIII.
SOFTLY AT DUSK

A leaf fallen in the water
rarely lifted by the wind

SONG OF THE CONCH

Life
I'm greedy for you—
every passing hour
I love you more

you rushing away
like a heedless river
and I trying to hold
a robin in flight

Dear blue larkspur
will you bloom for me
another season
a day
an hour?

✦ ✦ ✦

Death
don't be greedy for me—
The more you wait
the more certain you are
I will soon be yours

Spread your moth-wings tenderly
not to disturb
the song of the conch

When this purple hour fades
into a mauve void
we shall embrace

And afterwards, who knows

JANUS MASK

A child under a tall tree
peered through the splendid crown
tried to touch the rays of sun

He liked to reach for the unreachable

When he grew up, he was called
many synonyms of failure:
Dreamer, Man of La Mancha
too steadfast, unwavering
out of step with his time

He tended to his ideals
and let Sancho Panzas
live out their day-by-day existence

his imaginings more real to him
than the brilliant days
and somber nights

the colors more vivid
smells more enchanting
people livelier, pronouncements wittier
life pulsating more vigorously

Nearing the end, he clasped his dreams
the uncut diamonds, tightly under his shirt

while the thousand-faced mask of life
laughed itself to death

BARCAROLLE

I want
no iPods, no iPads
no hard-rock—

no morphine
of this rock-hard age for me

When I go down into the deep blue sea
let me hear the Barcarolle

White sand will settle over me
hum the old fashioned melody

fit for one who didn't fit
the last page
of her history

SCENT OF SPRING

As young springy curls are more winsome
than silvery wisps
so is hope sweeter than wisdom

I warm my hands on the child's warmth
resting them gently on her head—

now older
she lets me imagine
I still shelter her

Outside, the clement air caresses evenly
this morning's bud
and the last night's wilting flower

The scent of spring
tiptoes
over cyclamen

JUST IMAGINE

On a splendid chestnut tree
late autumn leaves susurrate

discussing the matter
of life-and-death

Would you rather
fall or linger?

They sound foolish, human
as if there is a choice

AUTUMN CONVERSATION

November is tapping on my window
with its tiny rainy-day fists

The violins of Vivaldi's "Four Seasons"
speak in their autumn voice to
the scarlet leaves
that hang doggedly
to a plum tree

The leaves whisper back
Is it time to let go?

On a live oak
a squirrel leaps
from branch to branch
as if it were a dry day

ROSE OF SHARON

Evenings between us fade
without a good-bye

Unhappiness loiters
through a prism of red wine

A red rose spilled across
the white tablecloth

At dawn, a moth flutters by
brushes it mauve, says good-bye

The rose sighs, sheds some petals
turns into a rose of Sharon

I gaze at it, make it mine
A precious pantomime of love

IX.
WHITE MOTH INTERLUDE

It's time racing with life
I'm just a spectator

WHITE MOTH INTERLUDE

Like white moths the nurses in cornettes
swarmed along a polished green-tiled floor

They came in small shuffling waves
bestirred quiet, sleepy dens
dispensed their white-moth nursing
marking days with silent pendulums
of convalescence

In bed mounted with gym bars
I exercised vigorously, keen and young

Across from me, an elderly nun
blended with hospital bedding
her face too smooth for her age—
a white plant grown
in ascetic cloister cells
instead of open spaces

Unable to move or speak
she just looked at me
A tear wavered sliding down
her virginal face

I couldn't meet her eyes

Ashamed of my exhibition
of regaining health
while hers was withering
ashamed of the cruelty of my youth

But most of all, ashamed of
having seen her naked feelings
in a tear she wasn't able to wipe away

HOME TO OKAPI

The hour, hour, hour
this is the hour
of my mortality

A blast rocks the engine
the boat knocks about
under my shaky feet

the flooded planks bob
over the swell
washing my future away

The hour, hour, hour
a fist knocks
adamantly on the door

The boat trembles for me—
although helpless and hopeless
I'm not ready to leave

this tantalizing
and bewitching
hellish paradise

that a few hours ago
was a vale of woe
but in this lucid moment

it became a home
to an okapi
of rare and aching beauty

ON A CLEAR DAY

I breathe deeply on a clear day

There's more air in the air
gladness swells in me

The leaves tethered to stalks
sway eagerly in the breeze

This restlessness is life

♦ ♦ ♦

I dismiss all thoughts
take off my socks

let bare toes
revel in dewy grass

Hopeful as incoming tide
my body relinquishes

the heaviness of bones
whose density I don't miss

Leaves untether
from their stalks

flutter high
above the shadows

free

A GLASS OF BUBBLY

I am an apple seed
source of impossible aspirations
well of new impulses

I am changed
I am the same

✦ ✦ ✦

My dear! You can bear your own aging
but not the depth of my wrinkles

You own up to your weaknesses—
my frailty frightens you to death

Is this tenderness too much
or not enough? Have I been
on the mantelpiece too long?

✦ ✦ ✦

A fragile figurine shatters
the silence after
deafening

My life is ebbing
First the fringes fray
then the cloth itself

Down the vortex
I hold onto nothing
not even a straw
but I glimpse life itself

A magnificent life!
To you I raise a glass of bubbly
tickling the lips
dazzling me to the core

that shifts
with a barely perceptible quake

COAXING WORDS

To a poet, words are everything.
I fear I may be losing them. They say
the first to go are the rarely used ones:

>The picturesque, the exceptional
>serendipity, cirrocumulus
>harlequin, confessional.

How I pamper them
stick them into daily conversation
to kindly remind them they are valued
hoping they'll fulfill *noblesse oblige*
and stay with me.

I begin to sound strange even to myself.
Stuck up. Preposterous. Bizarre.
Who talks like that?

Speaking to myself *sotto voce*:
You have always been bizarre—everyone is
They only seem less so until they are found out.

There's also this stubbornness that shadows me.
A history of aggrandizing.

When I tended tomatoes in my garden
my children tell me I called them glorious.
The chrysanthemums whose name alone
should be grand enough
I declared effusive, and so on.

Exaggeration is my thing—it lends me wings
although at this humble moment a single
word comes to mind—longing:

>I long for the lanterns in the sky
>that insist on twinkling away
>for the sun sinking into forgetfulness
>for the water dwindling in my well.

There is comfort in knowing
that the stars grace the sky
even when it's clouded up

an eclipsed sun still brilliant
when seen from some place else
and there's always more than one brook
to quench thirst.

I run to fetch the binoculars
a celestial globe
a dictionary to replenish my well.

For the time being.

AN IMPASSE

An old man squints
sizing up the horizon
trying to read its shimmer

Two youngsters approach
Hey, what are you doing Mister?

The old man replies
I'm gathering wool

They laugh condescendingly
We can see that
Where are you from, Mister?

I am from the sage and thistle
at the edge of swaying fields

Oh yeah? Where are
these swaying fields?

A long pause:
I, too, would like to know

Ahhh, leave him alone
He is crazy

HOURGLASS OF TRUTH

An oyster in muddy depths
swallows a grain of sand
strains to bear
a pearl
pure
rare
The pearl hides
bides her time, waiting
for a diver and deliverance

X.
BAREFOOTED HOPE

Life lives in the sinews of the limbs
and the stubbornness of the heart

BAREFOOTED HOPE

Out for a free ride
on a moving floe
in Glacier Bay, Alaska
a solitary bald eagle
feigns indifference

His body remarkably still
his eyes
engineered to follow prey in flight
swivel and hone in
on the floe's deep crack lines

He sees them for what they are
pretends they are a part of
an icy-wilderness design

He has been noticing them lately
but would not confront his fears
a scared tenant
ignoring eviction notices

A meek kuk-kuk-kuk
then an angry screech

He flies away
but he always comes back
hoping his faith will alter fate

The loyal bird and I

BLADE OF GRASS

I speak with the words
that have already happened
or I think that they have
or they ought to have happened

They may also be the words
that should have never happened—
the ones on the morning news
that wrench my gut
leave me vexed, depressed, enraged

Enraged can be good—it wipes out
the pages of resignation clean
My anger has the habit
of remaining speechless

Find your voice
scream if you have to

I'll go to the garden
to find my words—

Leaves linger on branches
as long as they can
Encouraging

Flowers shed petals
prepare for birth
model faith
Inspiring

Better yet, I'll drop in on a meadow
fragrant with grasses
strewn with stunning wild flowers
whose names I never knew
or no longer remember

Looking them up in
an encyclopedia of plants
just fingering those pages
I feel more alive
and curious, almost young

Keep searching
seek support

My eyes catch
a patch of green

I pick myself up by a blade of grass
find the words, go forward

THE KEY

Shiny and potent
it opens and locks
admits or bars

To the key, blame and praise!

A ridiculous item
lost in the folds of a purse
or lying on a counter
thinking itself important

One key, indolent, vain
dreaming of power

Some hapless victim
locked out, bewildered
searches for the metallic gleam of a key

Will the Eureka happen?

If not, a defeat—
a call to someone
a neighbor, a spouse
or the smiling locksmith
who'll cunningly do the break-in

The hopes and fears tango
in the merciless grip of civilization

Thinking of a home
welcoming strangers
I pause
consider the risk

but the wizard in my hands
is already locking my house
with cold habitual care

spreading the promise of safety
from the palm of my hand
into my civilized heart

SCENE FROM A PRIVATE MOVIE

The two of them left the party together
perhaps for the same destination.
By now their umbrellas may be
nestling in the same majolica stand.

Then, perhaps not, a good friend thought
they might be speeding away from one another.

Some are destined to live alone
or worse, be left alone.
He pitied their lonely lives, his own tidy
nothing ambivalent about his nest
in the house where people and things
never went missing.

Hi, Honey, I'm home.

The silence answers with an echo
the glare of discarded hangers
the table not set
the answering machine dead.
No messages or too many?

Honey gone.

A white envelope reclining
on an empty picture frame
doesn't explain anything.

He sits numb, stares at
the merciless phone
struck dumb after thirty years of
Honey, I'm home.

He totters toward the empty bed.
The screenplay will have to change.
Tomorrow they'll talk it out
but not before he warns her sternly
against such foolishness—

there was never anything
foolish between them.
He'll be forgiving this one time.

PERPETUAL MOTION

Nesting in my chest
a bird of discontent

burrows ever deeper
crowds my heart

until it runs away
abandoning the limbs

to move mechanically
to their fate

Time, a great arbiter
chimes in

Devoted to action
the limbs

like the hands of
a clock

come around
dip and swing

After many orbits
they muscle up

and host the miracle
of perpetual motion

To a hopeful beat they'll sing
about precious renewal

Then my heart will hear them
and migrate home

CREDO

There are paths that defy time and space
The hands reach out and find what is lost
There is love born in a single glance

The splendid sun comes up
On the wings of the shy dawn
The stars shine on wandering spirits
And plants grow for the love of seeds

The genes persist through the millennia
My foolish, precious hope is
They will go on forever

I must believe these gnarled words:
Truth can survive inside a squiggly line
Understand it with your heart

May this poem be the trowel for truth

NOTES

◆ ◆ ◆

Author's Note: The hand of Time, ever present in this collection, has urged me to assemble and publish this second collection of my poetry. As information from the archives of certain concentration camps became more available to the public, I was able to learn more about the fate of my family.

The main purpose of this collection is to bring that knowledge to light leading me to realize:

> *Truth can survive inside a squiggly line—*
> *understand it with your heart.*

SLENDER REEDS [Page 1] – This poem was inspired by one of my favorite books *Siddhartha* by Hermann Hesse. On his quest for Enlightenment, the protagonist encounters an old ferryman who brings him across a river, known as the Parable of the Raft in Buddhism.

WHAT BAKA SAID [Page 10] – *Baka* means "grandmother" in Croatian. In this collection, it refers to my mother who was a beloved *Baka* to our children.

ETUŠ | ESTERA [Page 24] – My mother's younger sister who was murdered in Auschwitz.

ROZA | RUŽA [Page 26] – Ruža Lerinc, my mother's older sister who was a resistance fighter shot and hanged in occupied Aleksinac, Serbia by the Germans.

About Jasenovac: The infamous concentration camp, the largest in Croatia run by the Ustashe, the Croatian equivalent of the Nazis in Germany during World War Two. Sixteen thousand Jews were brutally murdered there, among them, the following members of my mother's family:

IZO | IZRAEL [Page 27] – her younger brother

MARCI | MARTIN [Page 28] – her older brother

FANI | FRANCIKA [Page 29] – the wife of Marci

ACO | ARMIN [page 30] – the older son of Marci and Fani

MARKICA | MARKO [Page 31] – the younger son of Marci and Fani

Special Note: The names of my family listed in the poem titles on pages 24-32 appear with the nickname first, and the official name second as they were identified in the archives of Jasenovac and Auschwitz.

MY OMAMA [page 37] – *Omama* is "grandmother" in German.

SACKS OF TAWNY WALNUTS [Page 40] – Vlado, Vladimir Križnić, my father's brother, who was a resistance fighter, also killed in Jasenovac.

ROOTS OF CAUTION [Page 42] – When "war" is mentioned but unspecified, it denotes World War Two.

NINA NANA [Page 50] – A traditional Italian lullaby that my father sang to me, I sang to my children, and later to the grandchildren.

UNDECIPHERED IN CAPUA [page 82] – *Mater Matutae* refer to the pre-Roman Oscan sculptures of mothers holding babies representing the Goddess of fertility and motherhood dating from 6th to 2nd century BCE located in Capua, near Naples, Italy.

TIEPOLO SKY [Page 91] – Giovanni Battista Tiepolo (1696-1770) was an Italian Roccoco painter of the Venetian School.

JANUS MASK [Page 108] – Janus is known as the Roman God of transitions, such as beginnings and endings, depicted on gates and doorways, also on coins with two faces looking to the past and the future.

BARCAROLLE [Page 109] – A song traditionally sung by Venetian gondoliers; also, an instrumental or vocal piece of music, the most famous being a theme from *Tales of Hoffmann* by Jacques Offenbach, evocative of the rowing of a boat.

HOME TO OKAPI [Page 118] – Okapi, a species related to the giraffe, is mostly found in the Democratic Republic of Congo. The okapi is considered an endangered species.

PERPETUAL MOTION [Page 136] – While the notion of a working perpetual motion machine has been proven impossible, it still fuels the imagination because of what it represents—the ideal of hope and continuity.

ACKNOWLEGEMENTS

◆ ◆ ◆

I offer my heartfelt appreciation to my family—my husband Simon, our children and grandchildren—for their love and inspiration for this project. This volume is my gift to them and to the members of our family whom I write about, to those I call the *Beloved Ghosts* who came before us, and whose memory we cherish.

I'm grateful to Robert Perry of Robert Perry Book Design for his invaluable contribution as editor, designer, artist of the cover image, and manager of the production and distribution process that brought my collection of poems to life as a book.

Special thanks to my poet friends, and the poetry group leaders who kept the doors of Zoom open and the lantern of poetry glowing:

Phyllis Klein at *Poetry in Conversation*

Charlotte Muse and Patrick Daly at *The Not Yet Dead Poets Society*

Mary-Marcia Casoly at *Waverley Writers*, Palo Alto

Diane Lee Moomey and Steve Long at *Coastside Poetry*, Half Moon Bay

Monica Korde at *Belmont Poetry Night*

Lisa Rosenberg at *Poets Night*

Ron Miller at *Cupertino Poetry Circle*

COLOPHON

◆ ◆ ◆

Cover and interior design done by Robert Perry
Robert Perry Book Design and Dutch Poet Press
Palo Alto, California.

Printed and distributed by IngramSpark.

Display and body text set in Centaur
designed by Bruce Rogers and Frederic Warde
in 1914 and released in 1929.

www.ingramcontent.com/pod-product-compliance
Lightning Source LLC
Chambersburg PA
CBHW061737070526
44585CB00024B/2708